Destiny Rose has been through tremendous hardships. She has been hurt, been in love, and in general had a hard go of life. She lost her father at just 24 years old and that started a rollercoaster of emotional trauma. She has been down; as low as you can go, and pulled herself back up a number of times. She is hopeful this book will help others to see they are not alone in a battle with depression and constant emotional pain.

I would like to dedicate this book to my fiancé and best friend, Chris Breeding, who has had faith in me, and supported me through the good, bad, and horrible. My family who has always believed in me. To my children Chris, Gabriella, and Alyssa, who are my world and my reason for pushing on; my very best friend Jennifer Webster who has always been there and helped me through a lot of my trials. Thank you, and I love you all!

Destiny Rose

LOVE, LIFE, AND HEARTACHE

AUSTIN MACAULEY PUBLISHERS™

LONDON • CAMBRIDGE • NEW YORK • SHARJAH

Ordering Information
Quantity sales: Special discounts are available on quantity purchases by corporations, associations, and others. For details, contact the publisher at the address below.

Publisher's Cataloging-in-Publication data
Rose, Destiny
Love, Life, and Heartache

ISBN 9781649793775 (Paperback)
ISBN 9781649793782 (ePub e-book)

Library of Congress Control Number: 2021916697

www.austinmacauley.com/us

First Published (2021)
Austin Macauley Publishers LLC
40 Wall Street, 33rd Floor, Suite 3302
New York, NY 10005
USA

mail-usa@austinmacauley.com
+1 (646) 5125767

Over the years, while dealing with my anxiety and depression, I have written poetry of *Love, Life, and Heartache*. I have been through so much in my life and I feel many can relate to the feelings and things I write about. If I can help just one person to not feel so alone in their feelings and what they are going through by sharing with others, I would feel like I have taken a step to help people overcome their own depression and anxiety struggles.

A Beautiful Awakening

I see your hurt I feel your pain.
When I see it in your eyes My tears fall like rain.

You've been in love twice And they ripped your heart out
too.
Why won't you give me a second chance To prove I'd
never hurt you?

I loved you then And I love you now.
I will stand by you 100% This I will always vow.

You are a good man Outside and in.
Why play a game you will lose?
Play a game you can win.

I would be there for you If only you'd allow me.
Here, I pour my heart out Why won't you look and see?
I read the words you have written And they touch my very
soul.
Why won't you give in To this very girl you know?

You know me better Than I may even know myself.
I know you pretty well
But you put my love up on a shelf.

And there it sits Just to rot away. An undying love
That will never go astray.

I said it once And I'll say it again…
Why play a game you will lose?
Play a game you will win!

I offer my very soul to you It is yours for the taking.
Come out of your nightmares Into a beautiful awakening.

A New-Found Happiness

Not knowing what to think, Not knowing what to feel, It's
been a very long time But this feels real.

The way you touch me And how you hold me tight,
I could stay in your arms All through the night.

The words you say to me, The things that you do, How can
I not help
But want to be with you?

In all of my days Nobody has been so sweet, I find it
completely amazing
How you swept me off my feet.

Just one slow dance That's all it took,
One tender glance And now I'm hooked.
Since I have been this happy It's been a long while,
I have almost forgotten What it feels like to smile.

Thank you so much For giving it back, For giving back to
me
The happiness I lacked.

You will never know How much it means,
I thought it was gone forever Or that's the way it seemed.

Always Meant to Be

I thought I was ready for this, But now I'm not so sure,
Everything has come from a good place With love that is
so pure.

The love between and mother and a child Should never
have been broken,
But eight years of her life, From me, they have been
stolen.

I asked for your help
You have stolen my child from me How could you dare?

You are evil beyond words, The devil in disguise,
You have abused my child With your poison and lies!

She thinks I abandoned her And never returned,
The memories we have made
You removed and burned!

I have never stopped loving And praying for my girl.
She is living in a world you created, Nothing in it is real!

I will continue to fight Until she is free,
Back with her family Where she was always meant to be.

An Angel to Me

The Lord has taken you To His kingdom in the sky.
You were ready to go And we all know why.

Raise your voice and rejoice; Cry those happy tears.
You're with your husband and son After all these years.

For all left behind We'll miss you, no lie.
But we know you're happy, You'll get your wings and fly.

You've lived a long life, You've completed your task.
You'd give your shirt off your back To anyone, if asked.

The reason we're born, For this moment is known...
It's the very moment
When your Father takes you home.
He takes you home to His kingdom, And there you'll
always be.
Happy and healthy... An angel to me.

Anger

You take my kids And you take my life.
Allow me to make it easy, I will hand you the knife.

What do I try for?
What do I have to lose?
You get the rope and tie the knot, I will use the noose.

Lord, what do you have against me?
What did I ever do to you? I guess you think it's funny
Well, Buddy, Fuck you too!

Pushing me inch by inch Until I finally fall.
Without my kids, I am nothing, I'm just nothing at all.

Well, I will play your little game But I will surely win.
You won't get the best of me…
THAT would be a sin!

You are supposed to be the best, The best that is out there.
But I don't see how Because you just don't care!

They tell me to have faith, What exactly is that?
Something they just expect me To pull out of my hat?

I had faith once But you ruined it all.
You take away what means most And expect me to stand
tall!

I've tried my best
To fix what went wrong.
But it's been one step forward And twelve steps back all
along!

I am finished
So you can kill me now.
I am willing to go Right now, I make that vow.

Back to Reality

So now, here I sit Just another day. Still missing you
In every single way.

Wanting to call you But know it's no use. You won't pick
up But what can I do?

It's been four long months Since the day you said
goodbye.
But I'm just as lost As to the reason why.

I hear certain songs And it breaks my heart. I still don't
understand
Why we have to be apart.

I believe in my heart We'll be together again.
But until that happens My tears will fall like rain.

With all the tears that have fallen There are still tears to
come.
I wish I felt nothing... I wish I was numb.

But it just won't happen, I have tried and tried. My hear is
still broken, My feelings I can't hide.
Four months and counting And I'm still holding on.
I just can't let go It feels too wrong.

I will see you again One of these days. And when I do
I will come out of my haze.

Back to reality, Back to your embrace. Back to the comfort
Of your loving face.

Battles

There are battles I fight In the silence in my head.
That day after day Fill me with dread.

Fear of not being good enough, Fear of never doing right,
Fear of losing everything These are the battles I fight.

Not doing enough While doing all that I can,
Trying my best
To not lose sight of who I am.

I'm a strong person Who has a heart of gold.
I don't sugar coat, I'm honest and bold.

Though, while I fight these battles I'm a frightened little
kid,
Face buried in pillows Making sure my tears are hid.
I scream in the silence, I cry in the night.
I pray to God
To make everything alright.

The pain that I feel
Is more real than you know.

I feel it way down, Down deep in my soul.

So please don't judge By what you may see.
I may be fighting battles, But I'm still just me.

Beat of My Heart

As I look at the sky It's never seemed so blue,
In all of my years, A love so true.

My dreams are sweet And filled of love,
I realize now
You were sent from above.

I should have seen it then But I truly see it now, My love
to you, I pledge, My loyalty, I vow.

My world without you Would surely be gray, My heart
would break If you ever went away.

So stay with me Until death do us part,
I'll love you forever With every beat of my heart.
By: Destiny Rose

Breaks My Heart

In your arms
Is where I want to be Forever and always For all eternity.

I want to go to sleep with you And wake up to you each
day For the rest of my life
Is what each night I pray.

I miss you all week Until Friday night Where in your arms
I feel so right.

Then Sunday begins Another long week Of missing you
As the days will creep.

Not sure how much longer I can deal
Not quite as important Is how I feel.
Sometimes I feel
You loved her more than me But when I'm with you
I find that not true to be.

It's just really hard For us to be apart It tears me up
It just breaks my heart.

Burning Hatred!

So many things Going through my head, Like the question of why?
Why ain't I dead?

I don't want to be here, I have just had enough, For the past five months It just gets more rough!

With people walking on me And treating me like shit, I've had enough of the games They are all fuckin' hit!

Just one more wrong And it's gonna be done,
No one will wanna know me They will all wanna run!

They will know to steer clear And stay out of my face,
I will no longer be the "sweet one" In all of my haste!

You fuckers think it's funny But I'll no longer take the bait, I promise you'll be running When you realize my hate!

My hate for the game That you players play, My turn is coming... I'll get even someday!

You won't know when, And you won't know where,
It will be happening soon So players, beware!

You better watch your step, You better tread light,
Because when it happens,
Your life will be filled with fright!

I will no longer tolerate The shit that you do, When the
day arrives
YOU won't even recognize you!

Continue to fuck with me
And we'll see who's laughing then, Here and now, I
challenge you...
I **DARE** you to do it again!

Closed

I want you out of my life, I just want you gone,
I wanna let go,
I just wanna move on.

You just can't accept the fact That I just don't care,
You want me to want you To always be there.

But it's not gonna happen, It's just not gonna be, You
mean nothing at all, You meant nothing to me.

The reason I called Was to simply say goodbye,
To close this chapter For obvious reasons why.

You trusted me with a secret That I'll keep until I die,
Though it would be so much fun
To ruin your life, right before your very eyes.

Oh, but don't you worry Your secret is safe with me, I'm
not the "Big Bitch" That you make me out to be.

I'm not the one Who is in the wrong, Everybody knows it,
They've known it all along.

They have seen how you treated me Like I was nothing at
all,
Am I supposed to cry and say, "I need you And without
you I'll fall"?

Hold on to that dream Because I'm doing so well, Now
that I'm away from you I'm completely out of Hell!

All you did was use me When I was trying to be a friend,
But I cared so much That I just couldn't see it then.

But my eyes are now open And I can see clear,
Here and now you vanish
"Goodbye" is all you'll hear.

This chapter is now closed And I can move on,
Far away from your childish ways Now that you are gone!

Closer to the Edge

Confusion is surrounding me And filling up my mind,
I thought what we had Has been gone and left behind.

But then you drop a bomb And say you have feelings,
Not knowing exactly what they are, Now we are stuck
with dealing.

Is it rebound for you? Unhappiness for me? We need to
figure it out But only time will see.

Take it slow, One step at a time, But how to explore
Going down this particular line?

I am with someone, While you are not,
You don't want to be a wedge, But we are stuck in a spot.

How to figure these feelings Without a slight wedge, Its
gonna drive me closer And closer to the edge.

I think I want to kiss you To see how I feel,
But then what to do
If these feelings are real?

Death

Feeling so alone And not sure why,
There are people all around But I just want to die.

To get away from here, This God-awful place,
Feelings of pain, life, and love All to be erased.

Erase my life,
It doesn't mean much, Just take me away, Away from this
stuff.

From this Hell that I live That people call my life, Take
my life away, Please, with this knife.

I don't want to be here Don't you understand?
I'm nothing to this world, Nothing but a grain of sand.

I rest upon this beach
Then the water sweeps me away, Never to be seen again,
Never by the light of day.

Death is like a friend to me That I really want to find, To
take my life away Would be so divine.

Feeling like a nobody, That is my life,
Please, please, I beg you, Take me with this knife.

Distance

The feelings I feel I just can't explain.
The things I'm missing out on Make my tears rain.

What happened to romance?
It's just dead and gone. I want to feel wanted
I want to feel like number one.

I crave the attention That you used to show. Where has it
gone?
Where did it go?

I love you so much And I just need to hear How much you
love me,
But it'll never happen, I fear.

I crave the cuddles And I love your kiss,
But I can't get enough Of these things that I miss.

When we make love
It's as close as we'll ever be.
But sometimes you feel So far away from me.

Do you think about me Like I think about you?
Do you love me
As much as I really do?

I need to feel connected, I need to feel you want me.
I need to feel the love, You've got everything I need.

But why do I feel Like I'm just not enough?
Why do I feel Loving me is tough?

I know that you love me And that you have for years.
But why do I have All of these fears?

We are meant to be, I feel it in my heart. But sometimes I
feel
We are miles apart.

We need to close this gap Between you and I.
I can't take the fears That in my heart lie.

I count my blessings Every single day.
I love you so much In every single way.

The fear of losing you Is more than I can take.
The thought of being apart Makes my heart ache.

I need to feel close to you, As close as we once was.
This distance I feel Kills me…it really does.

Easter Without You

I seem so lost And so very sad, Here, it is Easter
And I miss you bad.

I've had a hard time These last few weeks, Always
wanting to cry And losing a lot of sleep.

The kids are great But Chris misses you so,
Gabby is getting big But she just doesn't know.

I haven't seen them lately I work every day,
But when you're a single mom It just has to be that way.

The holidays are rough Since you have been gone,
Lots of people still have dads And it seems so wrong.

It's just not fair
You were taken too soon, You went so fast
Like the sun trading places with the moon.

I can't help how I feel It's just not right, You should be
here
With your family tonight!

Emotions Be Gone

I'm shutting myself down Today and from now on, No
more pain, no more hurt Emotions be gone.

To feel nothing more Is a relief to me, People say it's
wrong
But why can't they see?

I am just here now,
I float from place to place, I'm really nothing special But
just another face.

I just can't take Any more pain,
I don't want to cry But they fall like rain.

They fall and fall and fall, Yet, never seem to end,
The next time my heart breaks It will never mend.

So to avoid all the pain And all of the hurt,
I throw my emotions down They now become dirt.

I shut myself down Today and from now on,
No more pain, no more hurt EMOTIONS BE GONE!

Even If I Die

So much for luck, So much for prayers, So much for love
It just disappears.

I thought it was good, I thought it was real, I thought you
were it The one true deal.

But I guess I was wrong, What else is new?
Here I sit all alone What else am I to do?

You've taken it all, My strength and my hope,
Now here I am
At the end of my rope.

I took a risk
And put my heart at stake,
Now when I'm around you, My smiles you want me to
fake.

To act as if nothing happened
Like we've been 'just friends' from the start, I'm sure I
can do that

But it would tear me apart.
But for you I will try,
Anything and everything Even if I die.

Forever in Your Arms

It's going on two years Yet it doesn't seem that long,
Seems like only yesterday We laughed and talked along.

I'm going crazy without you here Just one more day would
be fine, I just pray the Lord above
Will grant this wish of mine.

I long to see your face And hug you one more time,
To talk to you again
And say the things on my mind.

To say I'm finally happy And things are going good, I'd
like for you to see my son He's growing like he should.

I know that he would love you Just as much as us all,
If only you had the chance to play I know you'd have a
ball.

I miss you so much It just tears me apart,
But I know one day you will come to me And it eases me
at heart.

I know you are up there Always looking down,
Shining your love in all of our lives From our big to little
towns.

Just wanted to say I love you And you're always on my
mind, I'll keep you forever in my heart Your memory will
never die.

Please continue to watch over And keep us all from harms,
Close and protected
Forever in your arms.

Go Back to School!

I thought you were different, I thought you were real,
But you treat me like everybody else has How does that
make me feel?

I must be stupid, I must be a fool,
If you want to play games, Go back to school!

The things you sold me, Were all a bunch of lies, You are
as bad as the rest Just like any other guy!

The things you said to me, The lies that you told,
How can you be so deceiving?
How can you be so cold?

Fuck all y'all
That think you're so cool,
If you want to play games,
GO BACK TO SCHOOL!

I'm done with the games! I'm done with the lies! I'm done
with you fuckers And your cold, cold eyes!

I Wanna Be with You

Life is so screwed up It barely makes sense,
It seems there is a barrier I can't cross A bulletproof fence.

You have a wall
That you built around your heart, I'm trying hard to break
through And it's tearing me apart.

You say you wanna be with me But lately I have my
doubts, Tell me, what is going on?
What are you talking about?

Yes, I am attached Though, I just won't say, I'll be able to
tell you When I know that it's safe.

Stop the mind games And tell me the truth,
Do you wanna be with me?
I wanna be with you.

I wanna be with you, You and you alone,
I thought you wanted me too Through the affection you
have shown.

Was that just me?

Maybe my imagination?

I need to know the road ahead How much pain am I facin'?

Tell me how you feel Before I get in too deep, Please tell me soon Before I take that leap.

That flying leap

Past the point of no return, Love will never happen for me When will I learn?

Please stop the mind games And just tell me the truth, Do you wanna be with me?

I wanna be with you?

I Will Never Lie

I would take away The pain if I could,
If I could promise it would Never happen again, I surely
would.

When I see
The hurt in your eyes, It tears me apart Way deep inside.

I wish I could tell you How much you mean to me,
But it would do no good Because you just won't see.

I would tell you how I feel
If I thought that you would care, But for you to give your
heart again Is something you just can't bear.

I want to hurt her
For what she has done to you,
If you only knew
That anything you wanted, I would do.

I can be what you want, I can be what you need,
Just like a beautiful flower Had started as a seed.

It grows a little more With each passing day, Just tell me
what to do Tell me what to say.

You drive me crazy With some things that you do,
But I don't mind Because it's all a part of you.

If you give me that chance, I can prove to be
The kind of person you want The kind of person you need.

With love so true It will never die...
I promise you can trust me I will never lie.

I will never hurt you This I promise, too, Anything you
ask of me
I will certainly do.

I am here for you From now until I die,
I will always be honest... I will never lie.

If I Lost You

I almost lost you One horrible night,
When I heard what happened, It filled me with fright.

When they wheeled you out Of the trauma room,
I completely lost it,
It filled my heart with gloom.

What would I do If I ever lost you? I'm telling you now,
It would tear my world in two.

When I close my eyes I see you there,
Just lying there helpless, Like a bad nightmare.

I almost lost you One horrible night,
It scared me to death To hear you put up a fight.

I love you so much What would I do… What would I do
If I ever lost you?

I'm Missing You Badly

I'm missing you badly Each and every day,
I sit and wonder Why you went away.

Did I do something wrong? Was it something I said?
Sometimes I think I'd be better off dead!

Why do I bother? Why do I care?
We agreed long ago it was over, but I just can't bear To
live in this world alone
I realize now that I need you there.

I need you there To hold me,
To comfort me,
And to tell me what I need to hear.

I see you everyday But it's just not enough,
Though I keep telling myself That I need to be tough.

I can't let you see
How much you're hurting me, And no matter how much it
hurts, I should just let you be.

Those words you said to me Cut me like a knife,
And every day I realize more That I need you in my life.

You're the one that I want, You're the one that I need,
And now you know
How much I grieve.

I'm missing you badly Each and every day,
And there's so much more
I just can't bring myself to say.

It's Just What You Do

I've held on too long, It's time to let go,
And you have given me the strength For me to do so.

It feels so good... Not as hard as it's been,
But I need you to understand My heart is on the mend.

When you came in my life It was an easy choice to make,
But I am still very scared Of yet another heart break.

I know that you are too
And we can help each other through, After all, when you
are with someone It's just what you do.

To be there for one another And standing by their side,
To hold them close and wipe away All the tears they have
cried.

Be easy on my heart, It's still a little sore,
Continue to stand by my side And it will hurt no more.

Be honest with me... I will be with you,
When you truly want someone... It's just what you do.

Leave You Behind

I'm told you're coming home In just another week,
I was so happy and hoping You'll sweep me off my feet.

I can see the way That things should be…
You'll come home
And right away come see me.

I'll stand there in shock 'Cause I just didn't know Exactly
what day
You were gonna show.

You'll open your arms And I'll run to you, So very fast
You won't know what to do.

You'll say that you missed me, And then I'll show you
Exactly how much I've missed you too.

That is how
I feel it should go,
But I know I'm crazy 'Cause you probably won't show.

Then I'll come out of this dream Into this nightmare I live,
And forever wonder Why you just won't give.

Why you won't give in To the feelings you once had,
Through our whole relationship It was never bad.

Why did you turn And run away from me? I know it's not
the reason
You'd like for me to believe.

It just made no sense The reason you told me,
Just give us another chance And, I know, you'll see.

We were good together, We would never fight, We were
almost perfect
And, oh, so right!

Just tell me what happened So I can ease my mind, And if
I really must,
I can leave you behind.

Let Me Love My Man

Part of me loves you, I know I always will,
I can forgive the pain you caused But I will never forget
the feel.

The feel of the tears
As they rolled down my cheeks, Or all of those nights
I cried myself to sleep.

Wondering what happened, What did I do so wrong,
Feeling my heart break in two
It was with me, where you belonged.

Or so I thought
At that particular time, I managed to heal
And finally quit crying.

Now, here you are Back in my life,
You called to tell me You're divorcing your wife.

Then out of nowhere Come the words, "I love you." But
I'm happy where I'm at
I started my life anew.

I have a good man And he treats me like gold, I will
forever stay with him Until I am dead and cold.

I have finally moved on And left you behind,
It took quite a few years… It took a really long time.

So please leave my heart As much as you possibly can,
Let me be happy… Let me love my man.

I want us to stay friends And leave the past at bay, Just be
happy for me That is all I have to say.

Lies You Have Spoken

Think of me today, Dream of me tonight,
Come back to me tomorrow Let's make everything right.

You held me in your arms And told me it's forever,
I never would have thought That forever would be never.

How stupid was I
To believe your every word?
Honestly, tell me, Could I be more absurd?

Was everything you said Nothing but a lie?
How could you love me Then leave me here to cry?

I believed in what you said When you said you'd never
leave,
I trusted you completely But all you did was deceive.

I told you of my fears, How terrified I am,
But you used it against me And never really gave a damn!

You broke my heart, Ripped it right in two, And all I did
Was honestly love you.

You are obviously not the person That I thought you to
be...
I thought you to be honest and caring I thought you really
loved me.

But now here I sit, Alone and broken, All because of you
And the lies you have spoken.

Love and Life

Never regret love
Or you regret the life you are given, To have loved
someone Makes life worth livin'.

Love is something precious In life that you hold dear,
Love is hard to come by So grab it and hold it near.

When love is real and true You will have no doubt,
It is something you just feel Inside and out.

When you fall in love Your heart feels whole, Your life
feels complete
And it is then that you know.

Love is something special in life That two people share,
So when you find that someone Be sure to tell them you
care.

Be sure they know you love them And could never be
without, After all, finding love in life
Is what it's all about.

Meant All Along

How did we get here? How did this come about?
Ten years ago
We thought it was ruled out.

We came close once But something went wrong,
Now all is forgiven Maybe we were meant all along.

I am happy with you
Now we found each other again, Our past relationships
forgotten No longer to feel any pain.

You are good for me And I am good for you,
Since we found our way back We're stuck together like
glue.

You love my kids
Just as much as you love me,
It's wonderful to know Still very hard to believe.

Hard to believe We are together today,
We didn't think it possible But somehow found a way.

Still a little scared
But it will soon come to pass, Everything is going good
I am certain we will last.

I see your blue eyes Looking back at me, I know not to
worry
We'll just wait and see.

We feel safe and secure, This is right where we belong,
Together forever
It was meant all along.

Missing, Loving, Thinking of You

It's going on three years Since you have been gone, And
it's still very difficult For me to move on.

My son is turning three In just two short months, I wish
you could see him He has grown so much.

He talks so much And is very polite,
Everything I have done I must have done right.

I am getting married In just six months,
I know you will be there It will mean so much.

I wish you could meet him,
He is wonderful and kind, I know you would like him
This wonderful man of mine.

I am very happy, I know you are too,
And I am always here Missing, loving, and thinking of
you.

My Daughter

I feel guilty
For placing her where I did, I feel angry
For all the shit they said!

I feel hatred
For all the things they've done, I feel sad
For them making her feel so wrong.

Wrong for reaching out
To the true family she once had, Them getting angry
And making her feel bad.

Making her feel
As though she has no right, And then to tell her
SHE started this fight!

They tell her I will "steal" her, She will never see her
again,
Tell me, what is the point To cause her so much pain?

You have had her All of these years,
Only to fuck with her head And cause so many tears!

I pray the Lord help heal her And help her forgive as well,
As for me, all I have to say,
I hope you rot in Hell!

My Little Baby

You are so very small But growing very fast, I treasure
these times
For I know they won't last.

Soon you will crawl Then walk all around,
Running to show Mommy New treasures you have found.

Time is flying by Just all too quick,
You are getting so big In just lickity split.

I wish I could keep you Small a little longer,
But I know you need to grow And get even stronger.

You will be my little baby No matter how big you grow,
I am telling you this Because this you need to know.

I love you now,
And in years to come still, I love you forever And I always
will!

Nobody but You

Feeling very empty And feeling so alone, I sometimes
wish
My heart was that of stone.

I would feel nothing So I could hurt no more,
Reliving the last day That you walked out my door.

Not knowing you were leaving And not coming back,
Then finally realizing
That my world has gone black.

Willing the pain to go away And never to return,
And then kicking myself For when will I learn?

But the pain is still there, As fresh as that day
When you turned from me And simply walked away.

With no explanation, No reason as to why,
You said to me, "See you in a bit." Oh, why did you lie?

I cried so many tears, I just can't explain, Why after two
months

I still feel so much pain.
I wish I could forget you But my mind will not,
I wish I didn't love you But my heart does a lot.

Although, I know I shouldn't I will forever await your
return,
My heart will belong to nobody else For you, it will
always yearn.

With a love so deep, A love so true,
A love that burns for no one… Nobody but you.

So in my heart You will always be, My one true love
Forever a part of me.

From the very first moment, To our very last kiss,
I will love you forever Please, remember this.

I will never give up hope
That you will come back through my door, Wrap your
arms around me
And I will hurt no more.

One More Night

Nobody ever sees The tears that you shed,
Nobody ever knows Your feelings of dread.

But everyone sees The smiles you fake, And you can sure
bet
They see your mistakes.

Nobody knows How hard you fight, To make it through
Just one more night.

To get out of bed In the morning is hell,
Nobody knows What's under your shell.

The daily struggles Are hard and real,
Nobody knows
Just how worthless you feel.

Keep that smile, Fight that fight, Soon you will heal, It's
one more night.

Trust in God

And know He has a plan, For one day, you will see He'll always have your hand.

He will lead you through darkness And into the light, Keep that smile, Fight that fight!

One day, you will shine As bright as the sun, The darkness will clear
And you'll know that you've won.

Depression won't get The very best of me, I'll come out on top Just you wait and see!

So keep that smile, Fight that fight, Soon you will heal... It's just one more night!

Open Your Heart

Open your heart And hear what I say, The words that I say
Every single day.

You are my heart, You are my soul, You are the only one
Who makes me whole.

I love you now
And that will never change, You've shown me love
In so many ways.

I miss you more As the days go by, And every night
I look to the sky.

I wonder if you Are looking too,
To tell you I am here Is all I can do.

The reason you left I may never know,
But I feel you'll be back And it fills me with hope.

It may be months But I'll still be here, Ready and willing
To dry your tears.

You've shown me how it feels To have somebody care,
I miss running my fingers Through your blond hair.

I miss the feeling
Of your arms around me tight, I miss the feeling
Of your body next to me at night

I miss the feeling of your lips When you kiss my neck and
face, I miss the feeling I get
When you make my heart race.

Every time the phone rings My heart skips a beat, Hoping
that it's you
With a very sweet treat.

The treat that says You are coming home,
That you miss me too much, You can't bear it alone.

I hope things are well And that you are okay,
But please know I love you And miss you every day.

For now, all I do
Is count down the days, Until you come to your senses
And home, you're on your way.

However long it takes I'll still be right here,
When you come through my door And I can finally hold
you near.

Open your heart And hear what I say, The words I say
Every single day.

Pain

Emptiness and loneliness Is all of who I be,
The one person I want and adore Will never really love
me.

He will always be there When I need him, I know, But
when it comes to love It's a dead-end road.

So why do I let myself get hurt?
Why do I hold on so tight? Why when I feel it's wrong
Does it also feel so right?

Where do I go? What do I do?
I can't stop the way I feel, I can't not love you.

You have been hurt In a very bad way,
But I hope to help heal your pain, It will happen one day.

You will hurt no more, You will love one more time, She
will be a lucky woman And everything will be fine.

Shame

Where is my life going?
Why does it seem the wrong way?
Your life and my life
Are as different as night and day.

I miss you dearly, I really do care,
But the feelings that you want from me Right now, just
can't be there.

Afraid of commitment?
That may be why, But I need to be sure So I look up to the
sky.

I try to find direction
In the way the clouds move, 'Cause lately, it seems more
difficult
To go with the groove.

I've searched for answers At the bottom of every drink,
But one after another They leave me on the brink.

On the brink of destruction To myself and those around me,
I'm not sure what I want Though it should be easy to see.

And as complicated as I am I still don't see Exactly what it is
That you see in me.

I want to be with you And then I don't,
I want to be in love with you But then again, I won't.

I know that you love me As deep as love can go, It may be easier for you To just go with the flow.

To find comfort in yours arms Is just what I crave,
To fight along beside me And know my life you saved.

But, what is wrong with me?
Why can't I submit
To the feelings that I know are deep inside
From the flame that you have lit.

Just give me more time It will work itself out, I'm pretty sure it will,
I don't have much doubt.

You are good to me And a very good man,
Forgive me for what I've done I'm sorry, I really am.

I care for you too much To risk hurting you more,
I would completely understand If you walked out the door.

To walk away Just one more time, Not ever look back Or turn on a dime.

I'm so very sorry For causing you pain, Forgive my stupidity And let the clouds rain.

Release me from my shame That I now feel, God, bless his heart And please help it heal.

Somebody

My dreams are crashing down around me, My world is
caving in,
In everything I try to do I always hit a dead end.

Just when I think Things are going good, It never turns out
The way that it should.

When I am feeling low And need somebody there, The
one person I reach for Turns and disappears.

Friends are supposed to be there In your time of need,
Not to knock you down But to pick you up indeed.

I feel like a nobody, Like I mean nothing at all,
Why am I here?
Lord, just let me fall!

But determined, I am, And I don't know why, But I won't
give up
No matter how hard people try!

Kicking and screaming Every step of the way, "I'm gonna
be somebody,
I will be somebody one day!"

For all who said I couldn't, And those who said I
wouldn't,
Surprise, surprise, you all will see,
This nobody will become somebody **INDEED**!

Standing Tall

The feeling of being broken, The feel of complete defeat,
Has really worn me down, And knocked me off my feet.

Now what to do?
I've completely lost it all,
All my efforts of good, hard work Did nothing but cause
me to fall.

I fight and I fight With no reward,
But being blocked at every turn With barricades and
boards.

Well, they won't get the best of me I will be damned!
I will show them all Exactly who I am!

They'll be sorry they messed with me, This, I will make
sure,
Nobody will kick me While I'm broken on the floor!

I **WILL** eventually make it And I'll fight 'til the very end,
This one thing I will stand for And nothing will make me
bend!

They can try and try To make me fall,
But they won't succeed I **WILL** stand tall!

Strength

I work so hard Every single day,
How much more can I possibly take Before my life goes
the right way?

Everything is screwed up, It's all going wrong,
I knew this would happen I've known all along.

But still I try To do things right,
I work all day With little sleep at night.

I am so burnt out
And completely worn down, It's hard to fake a smile
When all I can do is frown.

But fake it, I must Until things look bright,
Eventually they'll turn around And be completely right.

With little to no help I'm doing it myself, Stretching
myself thin And ruining my health.

I'll find the strength To keep pushing forth,
Finding what I'm made of, Finding what I'm worth.

It will work out One of these days,
I'll find the right path, I'll head the right way.

For now I know
I need to be strong, Keep moving ahead When it all goes
wrong.

God, give me strength To keep pushing on, When all hope
it seems,
Has diminished and gone.

Surround Me At Last!

Emptiness in my heart, Sadness in my soul, My eyes keep
crying And now I'm on a roll.

A roll downhill
To the deepest of depths, Seems the only way to seize Is to
openly welcome death.

Death surround me,
I'll welcome you with no alarms, Take me to my Father
To be wrapped inside His harms.

I'll be with my loved ones And friends whom have passed,
Peace will surround me… Surround me at last!

Take Me Back

Take me back To that special time, When life was great
And we were fine.

When my heart was full And my mind at ease, Take me
back
To that time please.

I want to feel his kisses, I want to feel his touch,
I want to feel the tenderness That I've loved so much.

I want to see his eyes, I want to touch his face,
Oh, take me back To that time and place.

I want to remember Every single detail,
From the very first moment To the last piece of mail.

Take me back to the laughter... Forget about the tears,
Take me back to the promising days Forgetting all the
fears.

Take me back To relive those days,
When life was perfect And the hurt gone away.

Take me back To that special time When I was yours…
And you were mine.

Taken for Granted

So many things that I want to say Running in my head,
But the words are all jumbled Waiting to be said.

I don't know where to begin Or exactly how to end,
My thoughts are all just tangled My heart, never on the
mend.

It breaks my heart to see People with their dads, They all
take it for granted,
The things that I'll never again have.

The birthdays to celebrate, The hugs that are so tight, The
"I love yous" every day, and the goodnights at night.

The phone calls to say hello, The laughter in their head,
They take it all for granted, But one day, it will end.

What I wouldn't give To feel your hug again, To smell
your cologne,
And here your laughter in my head.

They say to remember The good times you had, But when
I do that
It makes me more sad.

I know I will never Again hear you laugh, Or even hear
you yell
When you are really mad.

I miss all these things, The good and the bad,
I wish I could have it back, All the time that we had.

But it is gone Never to return, My heart is broken
I hope they all learn.

Never take for granted, Say I love you every day, Because
it is inevitable,
One day, it will all go away.

Hold them tight And remember it all,
One day, it will all be gone And you'll wish you could
call.

Just to say, "Hello, What's going on?"
You will pick up the phone And remember they are gone.

The Fight

I cry in the dark,
I scream in my head, Some days it takes all I have
Just to get out of bed.

I suffer in silence
For the fears that lie deep, I'm completely exhausted Yet,
find it hard to sleep.

I try my hardest Every single day, To be the best me In
every single way.

The best mom I can be And the best wife, too,
Though it doesn't seem enough No matter what I do.

I laugh through the pain, I smile through the tears,
I try so very hard
To push back all my fears.

You seem to be pulling away And I don't understand why,
I'm doing all that I can
What more can I try?

I'm completely at a loss, I don't know what to do, I love
you so much
I just can't lose you.

I should have known years ago, But, I swear, I know it
now,
I love you today, tomorrow, always, This, I will forever
vow.

Please tell me what to do To make everything right, Tell
me what to do
I won't give up the fight.

The Only Man

I see your pain with my eyes, I feel your pain with my
heart,
I know what she has done to you Has torn your world
apart.

But I'm not her, And she's not me,
I will forever stand beside you Look in my eyes and you
will see.

I am here for you In your time of need,
My love is a beautiful flower And you planted the seed.

It grows more and more With each passing day, No way
am I leaving you
Not any time… **NO WAY**!

I know you are scared to hear it But I must tell you
anyway,
I love you now, I'll love you tomorrow, I'll love you every
day.

I see my future With the kids, you and I,
Because a future without you Would surely be a lie!

I see your blue eyes Looking back at mine, And I know
not to worry Everything will be fine.

Just one more thing You really must know, Whenever you
touch me You make me glow.

From my head to my toes As bright as the sun, Look in my
eyes
And see you're the one.

You're the one that I want, You're the one that I need,
When I see that hurt in your eyes My heart starts to bleed.

I'm right here with you I'm **NOT** going anywhere, Want
you to know
My love will always be here.

Please don't be scared I'm giving you my soul, You are
the only man,
I know can make me whole.

The Secrets

The constant battle, The constant fears, The constant
worry, The constant tears.

The screams that go unheard, The tears that go unshed,
The fears that aren't expressed, The feel of total dread.

Depression and anxiety Together take its toll, It hides in
the shadows
Just waiting to take your soul.

It makes you want to scream, It makes you want to cry,
It makes you want to hide, It makes you want to die.

Do don't judge a book By the cover that you see,
The secrets lie within, The secrets lie with me.

Time

What am I feeling?
Where is this gonna go? I'm not exactly sure
But I'll be patient 'til I know.

I feel a lot for you
And it scares the hell out of me, I'm not sure how to feel
So I'll just wait and see.

I can feel you hurting And it kills me inside, I see the pain
That you try to hide.

But you don't have to Hide it from me, I'll be here for you
In your time of need.

I'll wipe away the tears, I'll kiss the pain away,
I promise it will get easier Just take it day by day.

You can lean on me When you need a friend, I'll be there
for you Until the very end.

I know it's only been Just a few days,
But I feel much closer to you In so many ways.

I love how you hold me In your arms so tight, I feel so
comfortable And it feels so right.

But we're not gonna rush it, We're gonna take our time,
To see where it goes
Or to the end of the line.

If we don't make it, And even if we do, Always remember
I'll be right here for you.

We will take our time And go very slow, We'll wait and
see
Just where it goes.

To Just Let You Go

For the last couple of days
I have been pushing rewind in my head, Remembering the
things we did And the lies that you have said.

You said we would always be together Nothing could
make us part,
You said you would always love me From the bottom of
your heart.

But now here I sit, Alone without your love, Hoping and
praying
For a sign from above.

Something that says It will be alright, Keep on trying,
Don't give up the fight.

I am on the verge Of going insane,
I need to figure out a way To rid me of this pain.

I need to get my life Back on track,
Get rid of this pain And forget that you're back.
Everything you said Was nothing but a lie,

There was nothing I could do But try and try.

Try to make you love me The way that I loved you,
And hope the love you gave me Was that of love so true.

But if it wasn't, Two things I could do, Just learn to live
with it
Or say a big, "Fuck You!"

If you don't love me Just pack up your shit,
Get and stay out of my life And that will be it.

But to tell you the truth, It is easier said than done,
I am fighting a battle
That just can't be won.

If you don't love me Please let me know,
So I can forget about you And finally let you go.

As much as it will hurt To tell you "No"
I will do what I can To just let you go.

Twelve Years Gone

Well, here we are Twelve years gone, Both of us
wondering Why it took so long.

Why it took so long For that very first kiss,
I guess we had to wait a while For it to be complete bliss.

I cared for you then, I care for you now, It seems so unreal
I have to ask myself, how?

How is it
We were there last night, Just lying together Wanting to
make it right?

Why didn't we get together Way back in the day?
Is there a chance now? Any chance? Any way?

I hope there can be With a little compromise, It was me
there, Saturday
I saw the passion in your eyes.

Do you long for me As I long for you?
I've wanted this for so long Do you want this too?

So now you know, And I told you true,
Just answer the question… It's all on you.

What Do I Do?

Someone I care about Seems to be pulling away, So the
harder I fight
To make him want to stay.

Am I wasting my time? Should I just let him go? See,
these are the things That I just don't know.

I'm falling in love with him, This is true,
But I just can't tell him
It would be the wrong thing to do.

I fear it would turn him away And he'll never look back,
Then my world of hope Would surely go black.

I may be paranoid But I can't be sure,
It's almost three months in And that's when they hit the
door.

I try to tell him
The thoughts in my head, But he just gets mad
For the things that I've said.

We agreed to take it slow This, too, is true,
But I'm falling for him So what do I do?

Just wait for him to leave, But pray that he won't?
Prepare my heart to be broken But hope that it don't?

It's so very hard For me to trust
These feelings I have But I know it's not lust.

The feelings I have Run deep and true,
My heart is full of love So, what do I do?

He has been good to me, That I can't deny,
But how much longer
Can I live this lie?

The lie of not feeling These feelings I feel, I wish I could
tell him What I feel is real.

But I will keep my mouth shut For as long as I can,
And pray he will eventually love me For the person that I
am.

I will never hurt him… Not in a million years, I will stand
beside him
Through his worries and his fears.

I pray that he Will come to see,
I'm nothing like her… She's nothing like me.

I will treat him good And always be there,
I will love him wholeheartedly And show him I care.

We agreed to take it slow, This is true,
But I'm falling for him So, what do I do?

What I Need the Most

Kiss me gently
As if for the very first time, Soft and slow,
Let your tongue mingle with mine.

Run your fingers Through my hair, Caress my skin So soft
and fair.

Move your hands over my body Exploring from head to
toe, Upper, lower, in between Anywhere you choose to go.

Treat me like I'm special, The only one you love,
Like every day you raise your eyes And thank the Lord
above.

Kiss my neck so sweetly Sending shivers down my spine,
Slowly undress my body 'Til I'm about to lose my mind.

When you think I can't take anymore Make love to me so
sweet,
Full of love and passion Until we collapse from the heat.

When our love making comes to an end, Please, just hold
me close
All night long
This is what I need the most.

What Is Love?

What is love?
Who really knows?
Is it someone who will be there Through your highs and
your lows?

Is it someone who will be there Until the end of time?
For all eternity 'Til the day you die?

Is it someone who doesn't care When you act like a fool,
And who will stand by you When you lose your cool?

Is it someone who will be there Through the good times
and the bad, And who will stand by you
Through the happy and the sad?

Is it someone who will like you For being who you are?
Someone who will stop you Before you go too far?

Is it someone who will like your ups And won't mind your
downs?
Someone who will be there When all you can do is frown?

Is it someone who will make you laugh When you are
feeling low?
Someone you can turn to When you have nowhere else to
go?

Is it someone who can be your lover As well as your best
friend?
Someone who will stand by you Until the very end?

To me, love is all of these things And so much more,
Someone who will stay When others walk out the door.

White Trash

I don't know what I'm doing wrong I don't know who I
am,
I feel like running far away… As far as I possibly can.

It doesn't matter what I do, It doesn't matter what I say, It
always turns out wrong In every possible way.

I give, and give, and give, Yet, get nothing in return,
Will I ever be able to say "NO!"?
Will I ever really learn?

I've let people walk on me And never gave a damn,
Well, I'm tired of being trampled on HERE I make my
stand!

I am a very good person Inside and out,
I always knew I was, Always without a doubt!

You have always cut me down Does it make you feel more
of a man?
After everything I've given to you I've done everything I
can.

I will find out who I am And just where I belong,
They see me just as "white trash" But I'll prove them to be
wrong!

Why Is It So Hard to Say Goodbye?

I don't know why, But I miss you so, But I do know why
I don't want you to know.

Because I want To walk away,
I don't want to hurt anymore It may be too late.

I'm not sure
I am strong enough; I know I have to be I need to be
tough.

It is so hard to say I don't love you,
Cause down in my heart I know it's not true.

I wanted you
To be in my life, I wanted so much To be your wife.

But now it won't happen, You hurt me too bad, But I still
love you
Isn't that sad?

I know I shouldn't Have fallen so hard, But I couldn't help
it
You caught me off guard.

But now it's done, I already fell
And now it's too late, You've put me through hell!

I miss you so much And I don't know why, Why is it so
hard
To say goodbye?

Words

Wherever I go, I will remember you. Whatever I do, I will think of you.
In a crowded place, I will see your face. When I am alone, you will be there.
When I feel love, I will feel that you care.
When I reach for something special, I will touch you.
When I am lost, you will guide me.
When I search for hope, I will find you there.
But when I give you my heart…you will disappear.
Remember these words that I write for you And you will see, you are loved by me.

Your Eyes Do Not Lie

I long to feel your touch, I long to feel your passion,
I long to feel your love Way beyond all ration.

Take me through the universe, Take me to the sky,
Take me all the way To ecstasy I can't deny.

I want to feel you hold me As if you won't ever let me go,
Take me way past reason Until you see me glow.

I love to feel you inside me as deep as you possibly can,
I love to feel your strong arms And know you are a real
man.

As you touch me and kiss me You continue to take me
higher,
Until nobody exists, but you and I And I am dizzy with
desire.

As our love making continues Way into the night,
I no longer feel it's wrong Now I know it's right!

I know what I feel for you I can no longer deny,
And you feel for me as I do for you... Your eyes do not
lie.

Your Pain Is My Pain

I see how much you're hurting And it kills me every day,
To see the pain in your eyes
For all the hell you pay.

The hell you pay for loving someone It doesn't seem quite
fair,
For you to love with all your heart And they not even care.

That's not the way it's supposed to be, That is just not
right,
For you to love with all your heart And still you lose the
fight.

I know how it feels;
You let your guard down, just this once, Your world
comes crashing down And you feel like a complete dunce.

That's how I feel Every time I'm with you,

It hurts so bad
But I love the things you do.

I know it's hard to trust, But try to trust in me,
I will never do you wrong This, I wish you could see.

I will do my best To ease your pain, Even though, for me,
There is nothing to gain.

That's what friends do, That's what friends are for, I will
NEVER leave you
Bound and broken on the floor.

My feelings don't matter This is all about you,
I will do my very best... I will do all I can do.

No matter what happens Now or in the end,
I will always be with you, We will always be friends.

CPSIA information can be obtained
at www.ICGtesting.com
Printed in the USA
BVHW051559041021
618094BV00010B/358